Pre-K Chronicles:
what happens in pre-k, stays in pre-k

Written by Stephanie Hamilton
Illustrated by Darrius Godfrey

Editing & Formatting by Roseanne Frank - rbfrank.com

Dedication

To Geraldine Richardson Bush,
for believing in me and always finding the time to ask how
my students were doing.

Well, Hello There!

Are you thinking about becoming an educator?
Are you thinking about being an early childhood educator?
This book is not going to give you a step-by-step guide to being effective in the classroom,
and it definitely won't help you get through walk-throughs from an administrator.

Nope.
This book is something you need just to brighten your day or for a good laugh.

I have been a teacher for ten years and, crazy enough, I have been an early childhood teacher
for all those years. Children are pure comedy because they simply do not have a filter and they
share everyone's business. Everything they do is literal, and they do not understand sarcasm.
The conversations I have had with my students have made my head spin and my jaw hit the floor.
Like, did that just happen? I can't believe I just heard that!
Wait, pause, what did this child just say to me?

Every day, I walk into my classroom tired and overworked, but these little people make my day so
much more entertaining. Teachers are faced with impossible situations and crazy tasks with, of course,
a deadline. I am always thinking, "How is this age-appropriate for my students? How am I supposed
to test twenty kids on all different levels?" Let's not forget; I have to throw in potty training as well.
Who do you think I am? SUPERGIRL? NO!!!! But when a student starts talking about
who-knows-what, all that overthinking goes out the window.

The stories you are about to read are real stories that have happened in the classroom. Teachers
hear about "relationships" and other random things that do not make any sense to an adult but to a
4-year-old, it sounds perfect.

These stories are from classrooms, the playground, specials and centers,
and every story is pure comedy.

~ Stephanie Hamilton
Early Childhood Teacher

CHAPTER 1
EYES AND EARS EVERYWHERE

Do you have a child that is always in your business?
Do they repeat everything you say?
I always ask my students, "Why are you in my business?!?"

They can't help it. They are always listening and lurking. I have to stop
myself and look around before I start talking. If you are in the kitchen,
look around the corner. If you're in the bedroom with the door closed,
make sure they not on the other side with their ear against the door.
Are you making a phone call? Yeah, make sure there are no kids
around either. You will be surprised how much a child can absorb
just from one conversation they overhear.

The reason why I know all of this is because they come to school and tell me
ALL of your business and I have to wonder, *why do you know all of this?*

KEEP YOUR MEDS TO YOURSELF

I had a little cold, so I kept a small bottle of Dayquil on my desk and this is what happened next...I get a message from a student's parent:

*"Dear Ms. Bre,
My daughter and I were out shopping in the medicine aisle and all the sudden my daughter screamed, 'MY TEACHER DRINKS THIS STRAIGHT OUT THE BOTTLE! SHE DOES DRUGS!' All eyes were on us."*

So, I called the student to my desk. *Julia, what was I drinking?*

You drink that! That's a drug.

*Julia, sweetheart. This is medicine so I can get better.
It's not drugs.*

Oh, I thought you do drugs like my daddy.
My daddy can't stay with us anymore.

Oh, wow, yeah. Please go play now.

And Julia skipped away like nothing happened.

Bottom Line: I learned, from that day forward, do not keep any type of medicine on my desk.

WHAT HAPPENS AT HOME
SHOULD STAY AT HOME

I asked my teacher assistant if she could please pass me the rubbing alcohol to clean the whiteboard. And this conversation followed...

Can you please pass the alcohol?

Student 1 - Hey, my mom and dad have that at home.

Student 2 - That's not what my mom drinks.
She drinks beer.

Whoa, there! I am talking about rubbing alcohol, not whatever is in your house.

Student 1 - I know she drinks something in a red cup
every night.

*Yeah, no. We are not going to talk about this
ever again.*

SHOW & TELL

It's Show & Tell day, and the teacher and parent are talking about how the mom was in a car accident and that she flew through the windshield.

But that is not what the student told the class for Show & Tell...

Ms. D! Ms. D! I have something to tell you! My mom and dad got into a very big fight!

Really?!?

Yes! My dad came after my mom with a knife and cut her arm open and blood was everywhere!

Really? So, she was in an accident too?
She had a hard week!

NO! You're not listening! There was no accident.
My dad hurt my mom!

AND NO MORE TALKING! SHOW AND TELL IS OVER.

Students: AWWWWW, the story was getting good.

TELEVISION

Kids are not supposed to watch television shows that are not age appropriate. They will copy every word they hear or act out everything they see...

Ms. H, when I was little, I had a big brother and we played.

That's really cool. What did you play?

We played guns! We saw this tv show and they were playing with guns and shooting bad guys.

Oh, really? Did you have fun?

No. He pointed a real gun at me.

Wait, what?

So many questions ran through my head.
Where did the gun come from?
Why was the gun accessible to a child?
Where were the parents?

Now, you also have to realize that kids are excellent storytellers so, honestly, I did not know if the story was real or not.
So, I went on with my day.

YOU WATCH WHAT?

Let's get on the carpet to watch our video.

RJ: Are we going to watch *Love & Hiphop*?

No!!! Wait...why do you watch that?

RJ: I just do. You should watch it!
It's a very good show.

SIGH

IN THE CAR

Just imagine you and your child are driving down the highway. Both of you are having a great time singing songs and just talking. You don't realize you are speeding and out of nowhere ...

WHOOP WHOOP... a police car pulls you over.

[I'm at my desk looking at the lesson plans.]

Susie: My mommy got pulled over by the police yesterday on our way home but she didn't get a ticket.

Why? Why she didn't get a ticket?

Susie: She just told the officer she didn't have the money.

Y'all have to stop telling me your parents' business.

RED SOLO CUPS

Parents, you have to stop telling your children crazy stories. Teachers everywhere are wondering where in the world they are getting these stories from?

Children are so curious. You never know. They might sneak a drink from your cup because you said it tastes good. They might try to do something because it was perfectly fine for you.

Yeah, be careful parents.

WHAT'S IN YOUR CUP?

My Mommy drinks wine.

I'm sure she does, I say with a laugh.

**Nobody asked her anything about her mom
but if I had to guess, I am sure she brought that up because she saw
me drinking sparkling juice.**

CHAPTER 2
RANDOMNESS. IT'S OUR NORMAL

Have you ever had a conversation and all the sudden you turn your head and hear a small voice adding in their two cents?

"Who was talking to you?"

Children today are so grown-up. They think they are supposed to talk when grown-ups are talking. When I was growing up, I couldn't be around grown-ups or participate in their conversations.

In the classroom, you experience something off topic every single minute. Half the time you cannot even finish a lesson because, suddenly, you are talking about outside, dogs, or ice cream. You have no idea how often a lesson is redirected because a child said something WAY off topic, and now you have to engage because all the students are talking about a dog or a toy everybody wants.

TESTING

Testing students in the classroom is exhausting but it has to be done, unfortunately. This process can take up to two weeks. These tests are so repetitive, and its gets tiring because you are asking the same thing over and over.

There is always one student that makes your day because of the answer they give you. This is a conversation between me and a student…

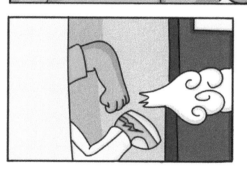

NOT WHAT YOU EXPECT

At the end of the day, all students are getting ready to go home. Everyone has their backpack on and they are on the train ready to walk out of the door. You hear their conversations and you just think to yourself, "It's so cute, the way they talk to each other."

But there is always one student that has to talk to you...

Annie: I used to be pregnant with my mom!
Wait? You!?
Annie: Yes, how else do you think she got here?
Um, Lol. (looking extra confused)

****

Playing games is a part of growing up, and they are playing games that we used to play as kids.

But sometimes I forget about those certain games...

Student: I'M GOING TO CUT YOU!!!
Me: (turns head quickly) *OH, NO YOU'RE NOT!!!*

Come to find out they were just playing rock, paper, scissors.

OTHER ACTS OF RANDOMNESS

The clouds are crying!!!

When he said that, I have to admit, it took me a long time to realize that he was trying to tell me that it was raining outside. I just don't speak small child. Honestly, I have never heard any student say that in all my years of teaching.

King: Do you speak Spanish?
No, do you?
King: Duh, I'm Mexican.
Really? Say something in Spanish..
King: Ummmm.
Yeah.

Why do students say they are allergic to something when they do not want to eat or drink something? JUST DO NOT EAT IT!!!

I am allergic to milk!
Really now? Are you sure because you were drinking milk this morning?
I just started to be allergic!!!!
[I roll my eyes] *Please eat.*

Me: Man, you are such a little diva!!!
Jess: No, I'm not!!! I'M A PERSON!
JUST SMALL!

Ms. H, do you know why everybody is hatin' on me?
No, why?
'Cuz I got these new shoes!

Ms. H! I lost my voice!
But you're talking to me.
I can't close my mouth!
I'm confused.

Why do I go to a magnet school we haven't even learned about magnets?

WHATTT??

As a teacher, there are times when I am sitting at my computer, minding my business during center time and a random student comes up to me and disturbs my peace…

Ms. H, Are you African?
Ummmm, no. Are you?
Well, yes, as a matter of fact I am!
Girl, disappear from me!
Then she runs away laughing.

Taking a class to the bathroom is such a task. The kids play in the restroom, play in the urinal water, run up and down the hallway, scream in the restroom to hear their echo, and the list goes on and on. And let's not forget the student that takes **FOREVER** to come out!

Valerie: I have to potty!
Ok. Go ahead. It's your turn.

minutes past

Girl come on out the restroom!
Valerie: Ooooooo – just give me ten more minutes.
(She sounds like someone's grandma.)

Have you ever tried to ask a simple question to a 4-year-old? Let me tell you, trying to get an answer from them is like pulling teeth or talking to a brick wall…

Can you tell me your phone number?
12345678910
Ha! Ha! Great job!

Amy: Who was your teacher when you were little?
I had a lot of teachers growing up.
Amy: Hmmmm, that's really interesting.

CHAPTER 3
DID YOU HEAR THAT?

Going outside during school is literally the best time ever for a 4-year-old. They can pretend to be anything they want to be. If they want to be a ninja turtle, go ahead. A princess in a castle? Go for it.

They run out those doors like they have been released from prison. You walk around monitoring to make sure they are not hurting each other. Then, of course, your head turns because you either see or hear something that is WAY out of order.

ADULT TRANSPORTATION

Bikes are an important part of a child's motor development,
so why not ride a bike?

HANDS TO YOURSELF!

Jasie: Ms. H! He touched me on my arm.

Ok.

Jasie: He touched me on my arm!!!

William: Snitches get stitches!!!

Whoa, there...let's take an entire break.

★★★★

Ms. Hamilton, Jimmy hit me with a toy.

Why would he do that?

He hit me.

But why?

He hit me like this. (Hits me with a toy)

Yo! Why did you hit me? I know what hitting is!!!

(The student proceeds to laugh and walk away. *I hate it here.*)

NO BUNNY'S BUSINESS

Normally when we're outside, teachers are really just minding their business talking to other teachers and taking a little adult time.

Until something like this happens...

Moral of the story: 4-year-old's take everything literally.

WHEN A NOTE HOME IS REQUIRED

Parents, please be mindful of what you say to your children. Children do not have a filter and will tell everything!

Student: (taps the teacher's leg)

Teacher: Can I help you?

Student: She's wearing a crop top.

Teacher: Is that bad?

Student: Yes. Mommy said little girls who wear crop tops get "got."

Teacher: *Gets "got"?*

Student: Yeah, she get hurt. Only grown-ups can show their tummy.

★★★★

[Children playing with wood chips under the slide.]

Student: Pass it.

Student 2: Not your turn yet.

Teacher: *(Hears the conversation and decides to walk by them)*

Student: You not hitting it right!

Student 2: Yes, I am I know how to smoke.

Teacher: *PAUSE!!! WHAT ARE YOU TWO DOING?*

Students: Smoking like our parents!!! Duh!

Teacher: *IT'S TIME TO GO INSIDE!*

Students are playing in the gravel with their Tonka trucks. That's innocent enough, right?

Student: *(found a sandwich bag)* How much you want?

Student 2: How much you got?

Student: Let me weigh it. You owe me a dime.

Student 2: Ok, I got that. *(Pretends to take money out of pocket)*

Teacher to teacher: *I think he just sold her drugs.*

Teacher 2: *Nope. I saw nothing.*

Yeah, best believe notes were sent home.

BUT THEY'RE JUST SO DARN CUTE, TOO

Alex don't want to play with me.

Well, today he wants to play with his cousin.

He can't!

Why not?

HE IS MY BEST FRIEND!!!

Alex! Please come here. Please play with her.

I can't. I'm playing with Bobby today.

You have two hands, so she can hold that hand.

No, that hand not clean for her.

Should I ask why?

I was playing in my nose.

GO WASH YOUR HANDS.

At least he was being considerate.

Every once in a while, the students want to play with the teacher. Sometimes the teacher will actually go along with it.

Ms. H, I want to race today.

OK, I guess I can do this.

LET'S GO!

READY, SET, GO!!!

Students all run but one decides to take a big u-turn.

I won, I won!

You cheated, though.

It's ok 'cuz that's the only way to win.

Sometimes the weather does not want to cooperate and, of course, that means having to stay cooped up inside with 15 PreK students.

It's bunderstorming!

Yes, it is.

Can we go on the playground? It's not raining on the playground.

Baby, it's raining everywhere.

Aw, man. So that means no outside time.

The grass is growing. Shhhh, we can't disturb it.

[All the students grab their jackets]

PRE-K PAUSE!!! We are not going anywhere

but we can go to the door and look at the rain.

Everything is so amusing at this age.

They sat at the door for 15 minutes looking at the rain.

Playing outside can be so tiring, so that's what I've been told.

I'm tired.

Well, sit down.

[The student grabs the teacher chair]

Oh, no ma'am. Sit on the ground.

Oh, never mind. I'm not tired anymore.

Apparently, sitting on the ground was beneath her so she'd rather run around and get even more tired.

CHAPTER 4
SAY WHAT?!

Being a teacher can be so exhausting but being an early childhood teacher can be downright draining.

Throughout the day I usually find myself saying some off-the-wall things. Then I think back to myself, *Did I really just say that?*

Kids at this age are very curious and very touchy-feely, if that makes sense. They want to touch EVERYTHING!!! They want to see how things work and what can happen if they do something.

A teacher's reactions can cause some surprising conversations.

Teacher: *Why are you massaging my hand?*

Student: Your hand looked stressed.

★★★★

Student: Why are wearing clothes?

Teacher: *Do you want me to be naked?*

Student: NO!!!! I don't want to see that.

★★★★

Teacher: *DID YOU JUST LICK MY HAND?!?!?!?*

(Student shrugs his shoulders) I don't know.

★★★★

Teacher: *Go put your shoes on.*

Student pees on my carpet.

Teacher: *IS THIS THE TOILET!!!*

Student: I thought it was.

This child literally had a full stream of pee hitting my carpet. There was nothing between the pee and my floor. I really feel like he was mad at me and decided to get back at me by peeing on my floor.

Twin A: I don't have a mom.

Teacher: *You don't?* (I turn to Twin B) *Do you have a mom?*

Twin B: Duh, I have a mom!

(Teacher – I look at Twin A)

Twin A: His mom is not my mom.

Teacher: *Y'ALL ARE TWINS!!!*

★★★★

Student: HE BALD!!!

Teacher: *No, he is not. He just got a haircut.*

Student: OOOOOKKKK. That's fine then.

★★★★

I never understood why little girls so young wear weaves in their hair, but I guess that is not for me to understand.

Student: WHY IS YOUR HAIR OFF YOUR HEAD!!!

(A student's braid fell out and was currently on the classroom floor and a little boy found it.)

Teacher: *WHY ARE YOU LICKING THE TABLE?!?!?!*
Student: I don't know.

★★★★

This is a story from a parent who was traveling with her child and her baby.

Baby: (sneezes)
Mom: Bless you
Baby: (sneezes)
Mom: Bless you
Baby: (sneezes again)
Mom: Bless you
Child: Man, that is one BLESSED baby.

★★★★

Being stuck in traffic can be very interesting when you have small children in the car. Children can sense when the parent is frustrated.

Child: MOVE, BEEP BEEP!
Parent: (laughs) why are you saying that?
Child: WE STUCK IN TRAFFIC!!! MOVE BEEP BEEP!

CHAPTER 5
VIRTUAL SCHOOL + CORONAVIRUS (UGH)

Coronavirus has really taken a toll on keeping kids in school. So much had to change to keep the learning flowing. We have done all virtual, hybrid, and back to the classroom. May I just say, teaching virtual is absolutely TERRIBLE.

Four year old kids in virtual school? Who thought of that?
I can barely keep their focus when they are in front of me, now I have to talk to them on a screen.

Yeah, no.

I had kids sleep, get up and watch TV or – the best one yet – ask me if I'm done teaching. Let's not get me started on hybrid learning. They want me to teach kids in class and virtually...

AT THE SAME TIME!!! NOOOOOOO!!!

Teaching virtual school is tough and not for the weak.
Especially if they have siblings at home running in and out of the room,
or they're speaking too loudly in the background and then my student
can't hear.

Teacher: (plays video for students to watch)

OK, my friends. Can you tell me what letter we are talking about?

Student: CAN Y'ALL BE QUIET. I CAN'T HEAR MY TEACHER?!?!?

You tell them, CJ! You need to learn too. (laughing)

****

Have you ever tried to virtually test a 4 year old? I do not recommend it at all.
All throughout the test you have somebody trying to whisper the answers to
them. UMMM, I CAN HEAR YOU!!!!

Can you tell me what this letter is?

Nope Nope Nope.

Ok, then. Next subject…math.. What's this number?

Naw, nope, no. Can I go watch Paw Patrol now?

Awesome job, Jimmy!!! You may now go finish your show.

This was just 1 child out of 19 and it was the first day of testing.
Let me just say, that began a terrible two weeks.

So the in-class students are cleaning up their breakfast
and vacuuming up their crumbs.

As they do that, I am trying to get the virtual kids ready
to start the morning.

Then this happens...

To make y'all feel better I did give him a new, fresh mask and he
was excited that he wasn't dying that day.

Of course, this virus is changing the way we live.

We have a statewide mask mandate and we are forcing 3 and 4 year old children to wear them correctly.

Yeah, ok! (Sigh) Let's see how that works out.

Somebody please explain to me how he lost his mask in 5 minutes!?!?!
Yes, I did get him a new mask but the problem was I had to fish the mask out the toilet and put it in a zip bag with an awesome note home.

ZOOM!

Teaching on Zoom has its perks because now you can actually mute a student when they are talking too much. Yeah, that was the best function that was ever invented.

MUTING A STUDENT. GENIUS!!!!

So today we are going to talk about rules.
Can anybody tell me a rule you have at your house?

JoJo: I don't have any rules.

Parent in background: WHO DON'T HAVE RULES???
I KNOW JOJO HAS ALL THE RULES!!!

Ok, then. (mutes student). Craig, what about you?

Since the virus apparently just does not want to go away and we are now 100% back in the classroom, I have to find ways to keep me and my students safe. So, I set alarms for Lysol.

(Alarms goes off)

Students: LYSOL TIME!!!
Teacher 2: (walks by my room and peeks in)
Teacher: (sprays the entire room with Lysol)
Teacher 2: You train them to say that?

Teacher: *Nope, I do it 4 times a day so it becomes a routine with them. They hear the alarm and they know what comes next.*
Student: You don't spray in your room?
Teacher 2: No, I don't.
Student: EWWW, WE CAN'T PLAY IN THERE THEN!!!
Teacher 2: (walks away)

I couldn't help but laugh because we keep telling our students that germs don't like Lysol. So, in their mind, her room is full of germs.

Reading aloud while online is a very difficult task to do.
Can the kids hear me?
Is their screen on? Are they in a quiet place to listen?

So, I am reading a book and on one particular page a kid is chewing gum with their mouth open, and I decided to stop and discuss the page.

Student: TEACHER!!!! I can't chew gum because I swallow it.

Student 2: Yeah, my mom said no more gum because it got stuck in my hair.

Teacher: *I am grown so I love to chew gum. hahaha.*

That lesson never got done because for the next 30 minutes, we talked about gum and we never finished the story.

CHAPTER 6
COME TO THE WILD SIDE

If you ever walk into a pre-k classroom, you will see nothing but colors everywhere. You have to have an inviting room so the students will feel comfortable. You might see circle time, center time, small group, or testing.

At any given moment, you will see a child throw a fit or just have a complete meltdown. Students feel safe in the room so, therefore, you make some unbelievable connections with the students and their parents (unfortunately).

It's just a different type of love and energy, and if you do not feel that, then something is wrong.

SIDE NOTE: WE ARE NOT A DAYCARE.
WE ARE ACTUALLY LEARNING!!!

Good morning! I have missed you, CJ!

CJ: I know. I been ghost for a long time.

Ghost?

CJ: Yeah, you know. I've been missing.

Boy, where did you hear the word "ghost"?

CJ: (points to the teacher assistant)

(TA): I really need to watch what I say.

Student: (walks up to teacher)

Yes, how may I help you?

Student: (whispering) I hear friends in my ear.

(Teacher whispering) *You better go find those friends then.*

Student: Ok. Good idea.

Just think about a 3 or 4 year old child. You have been at home for the first years of your life and, basically, you have done anything you wanted and now your parents decided to enroll you in school and you have to hear the word, NO. Especially in my classroom.

I set the tone at the beginning of the year and I always make sure my students know that they are responsible for their own actions.

So, you can see how this can rattle a young child.
Like this...

CHAPTER 7
PARENTS: THE OVERGROWN CHILD

As a teacher, you always hear people say,
"Wow! You're a teacher. That's an easy job."
"Aww, that's so cute."
"You're lucky you have summer off."
And the list goes on and on.

People who are not teachers, do not understand what we have to deal with on a daily basis behind the scenes. I wish I can just go into my classroom and teach how I want to teach but, sadly enough, I can't because everywhere I turn, somebody is telling me what to do.

I have been in the teaching profession for some years now and I have to tell you, the parents I have had are some interesting people. You will have overly involved parents, missing parents, clueless parents, young and old parents. I have been yelled at, chased, cussed out, and so much more but the funny part is:

I WOULDN'T TRADE IT FOR ANYTHING!

ARE THESE MY ALLIES?

My first year of teaching was one for the books. I had no idea what I was going to expect for my first open house. My heart was beating fast and I was sweating. I was meeting all of my parents and I was doing pretty well until that one parent came in and all the alarm bells went off in my head.

Parent: What's up, Hamilton?

Me: *Ummm, Hi. (smelling all the drugs on her)*

Parent: I'm telling you now, he will have zero school supplies

and I am not going to buy any.

Me: O*oookkkk (not surprised)*

Parent: Why are you not surprised by how I'm acting?!?!?

Me: *(silence)*

(Parent hits my arm, playfully) We going to have a great year with you!

(Turns and leaves classroom)

Me: *Oh, boy.*

(And at that moment, I was rethinking my life choices.)

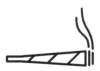

**There is a rule of thumb that when a student gets hurt in your class,
you call the parent and let them know.**

Hi, Ms. Jackson. I am just here to inform that your baby scrapped her knee in the hall. She was pushed and she fell, and she went to the nurse. The other child was punished. Everything is fine.

Ms. Jackson: Ok thank you. Did she cry?

She did a little bit, but I held her and she stopped after we left the nurse's office.

Ms. Jackson: Ok, that's good. Thank you. (hangs up the phone)

**I am thinking everything is all right and I followed everything by the book.
I am not sure what happened from the phone call to dismissal
but everything changed.**

Ms. Jackson: WHERE IS MS. HAMILTON!!! YOU HURT MY CHILD!!!
(proceeds to run toward me)

Now I am between fight or flight situation and I actually liked my job so, what do y'all think I did?

I RAN.

This little chasing scene went on for about five minutes before I turned around and yelled..

"Chill out. What is this about?!?!?"

Meanwhile, my principal is laughing extra hard and I'm just trying to catch my breath.

Why are you chasing me?

Ms. Jackson: I need to get your attention.

SO, YOU CHASE ME?!

This parent really thought we were hurting her child but in all actuality, her daughter was really clumsy and had zero social skills.
I can see where she got it from.

ARE THE PARENTS ALWAYS RIGHT?
I WONDER...

One year, I decided to leave the classroom and teach STEM.
This was the most fun I ever had in my career. Now let me remind you that since I teach every kid in the school, that means I have to deal with every parent in the school too.

Everything always happens at dismissal. I am in the gym trying to corral these 4 year old children so they can go home. They are supposed to sit down in their line and stay semi-quiet because, let's be honest, you can't get over 150 4 year old's completely quiet. Well, there was this little boy who was constantly screaming and wouldn't sit still so, naturally, I walked over to him and started talking to him.

Hey, buddy. Can you be quiet so your other friends can hear their names?
Jeremiah: NO!!! I WANT TO PLAY!
Well, this is not the time to play. It's time to go home.
Jeremiah: I DON'T WANT TO GO HOME!

So, I could tell I wasn't going to win this battle with him, so I decided to move him to the back of gym and what does he do? Goes completely limp!!!

Jeremiah, please get up. I don't want to trip over you.
Jeremiah: NO!!!

So, I'm trying to move him and I trip over him. What does he do? Cry.

Jeremiah, it's time to go home!

Jeremiah is still crying, and I put him in the car and explain to his mom why he was crying. I'm thinking that was the end of that...NOPE!

The mom pulls away and makes a U-turn and two women get out the car and stand on the curb.

Parent: YOU STEPPED ON MY SON'S FINGER ON PURPOSE!!!

Me: (Looking around. Who is she yelling at?)

Parent: I'M COMING OVER THERE TO BEAT YOUR A**!

Once again, I'm not moving because she yelling from across the street.

Ma'am, I did nothing to your child. I already talked to you so, what is your purpose?

This parent never walked across the street but continued to yell for five minutes and just walked away.

I am amazed how parents act when they are completely in the wrong. I swear, they just like to put on a show for whoever is watching. I know they say the parent is always right but at this age, they are almost 80% WRONG!

WE ALSO POTTY TRAIN, I GUESS

So, I had a new student come into my class about a month into the school year. I met her mom, and everything looked promising with this family. Man, I was so wrong about this one.

We were walking back from the cafeteria, and I just so happened to turn my head and notice that this child not only has on a pull-up but is completely soaked. Naturally, all these questions pop into my head.

Me to the Assistant Teacher: *Um, Ms. T. Is that a pull up?*
Ms. T: What??? I thought she was potty trained!
Me: *Me too because she didn't say anything about not being potty trained.*

I immediately called her mom.

Hi, Ms. Smith. I noticed your baby has on a pull up.
Yes, she does. Is she wet?
Extremely wet!
Oh, yeah. She not potty trained! Didn't think I needed to say anything because she four.
What?!?!? Ma'am this is something you need to let us know because all the students use the bathroom by themselves.
Oh, I thought you changed them all day.
(Thinking…what nonsense planet did she come from?) *Ummm, no ma'am. Our kids are potty trained and yours will be too.*
Really? You going to do that all by yourself?
Absolutely not! You will help so we can get your child back on track.

Long story short, she did get potty trained in two weeks and the mom absolutely had to help. What are we doing here?!?!?

TWIN PROBLEMS/MAMA PROBLEMS

What parent do you know worries about everything else
except their child's ridiculous behavior?
Yeah, it's like a disease running around the school.

I had a set of twins in my class, and they were literally one inch
short of being wild animals. They were everywhere, and every
day I went home exhausted and defeated.
And their mom did not help the cause.

Why is my son sitting behind the desk?
(*I realized she was on the class app looking at the classroom.*)
Oh, he got in trouble and he is in timeout.
We don't believe in timeouts at home.
*In room 101 we do, because they are not going to hit other students and
not get punished.*
Oh, yeah. He does hit but I just ignore it.
*That's not happening in here. We teach kids they need to be responsible for
their actions no matter their age.*
Well, theys just stupid!!!

Why is my baby sitting by the trash can?

Ma'am, what are you talking about now?

[I looked at the picture on the app and he is sitting by the trash can]

Ma'am, that trash can sits there all day, every day. He sits in front of the trash can because that is his circle on the carpet. The trash can is not bothering him and it's really not that close to him either.

You singled my child out! I want him moved out your class!

That's not happening. Every class is full and your request will be denied. Now we treat all students the same way no matter what. Some need extra attention and, in your case, your child needs the attention.

Ugh! I'm done talking to you!

Those boys stayed in my class all year long and the mom finally got on the same page as us. Sometimes you have to teach the parent more than the student.

Crazy how that works in the teaching profession.

RING! RING!

Well, that's about it – for now!

It's the end of the semester and I am just as ready for summer vacation as the kids!

I hope you enjoyed the glimpse into a pre-k classroom and why we love what we do.

I can't imagine doing anything else.
The children are definitely our future. All of our futures.

And how blessed I am to be a part of that.

ABOUT THE AUTHOR

Stephanie Hamilton is an early childhood educator with certification in Early Childhood through 6th Grade, and has over 12 years experience in the classroom. She attended Tuskegee University and has a degree Biology. She lives in Grand Prairie, Texas. During her free time, she works as a Ride Supervisor at Six Flags. Pre-k Chronicles is her first book. You can reach out to her at shamilton10187@gmail.com.

Printed in the USA
CPSIA information can be obtained
at www.ICGtesting.com
LVHW070723220823
755931LV00016B/319